We Can Sign!

ROCKRIDGE
PRESS

WE CAN SIGN!

An Essential Illustrated Guide to American Sign Language for Kids

TARA ADAMS Illustrations by Natalia Sanabria

For general information on our other products and services or to obtain technical support, please contact our Customer Care Department within the United States at (866) 744-2665, or outside the United States at (510) 253-0500.

Rockridge Press publishes its books in a variety of electronic and print formats. Some content that appears in print may not be available in electronic books, and vice versa.

Interior and Cover Designer: Liz Cosgrove
Art Producer: Michael Hardgrove
Editor: Barbara J. Isenberg
Production Editor: Andrew Yackira

Illustrations © Natalia Sanabria, 2019.
Author photograph courtesy of Carrie Hampton

ISBN: Print 978-1-64611-285-2
eBook 978-1-64611-286-9

R0

For my smallest students,
whose tiny hands remind me what a gift it is
to connect and communicate—
no matter the language.

Contents

Introduction

HAVE YOU ever seen someone signing and thought to yourself, "I want to learn to talk like that!"

Do you want to learn a second language? Do you love the idea of learning a language that enables you to talk without using your voice?

Are there Deaf or hard-of-hearing (hh) kids at your school, in your neighborhood, family, or community? Would you like to be able to include them in conversations and social events?

Do you like the idea of being able to talk across a crowded room or in a noisy environment without having to yell? Or perhaps you would like to learn to yell without straining your vocal cords?

Do you love challenging yourself and learning new things?

Do you want to prove to your parents that you *can* talk with your mouth full?

Do you know someone with special needs who struggles to express themselves verbally and uses, or could benefit from, signing?

Do you and your friends or siblings want to learn to talk with one another without others being able to eavesdrop?

If you answered "YES!" to any of these questions, then you have come to the right place.

Welcome to *We Can Sign! An Essential Illustrated Guide to American Sign Language for Kids.* This book contains everything you need to know to start communicating in a completely different way.

I'll never forget when I first started learning American Sign Language (ASL). I was fascinated by the way language came to life through signing. I loved expressing myself with my hands, face, and body language. As a person with hearing loss, I found that learning ASL opened up many doors. I finally had full access to language and a way to connect with others (which can sometimes be challenging for people with hearing loss and speech impairments).

I am a mother of two children who have hearing loss, so I am deeply aware of the impact a larger community of signers can make in the lives of kids. The more kids who know ASL, the more kids who are Deaf or hard of hearing (hh) will be able to interact and connect with their peers. (That means *you!*)

I've designed this book to make learning ASL easy and fun. It's divided into 10 simple chapters.

In **CHAPTER 1,** we explore the history of ASL and how it differs from English. You will learn the five parameters of signs, grammar basics, and the sign language alphabet and numbers.

In **CHAPTER 2,** we review general conversation starter signs and some common phrases to help you begin signing right away.

CHAPTER 3 introduces signs for objects and rooms found around your house, as well as signs for family members and pets. You will learn the reference points on your face to show male or female signs.

In **CHAPTER 4,** we outline action words and verbs. These will help you express what you are doing and make simple requests. You will learn about directional verbs and how to use them.

CHAPTER 5 is all about feelings. You will practice showing emotion on your face as you sign, as well as what it means when your facial expression does not match the sign you are using.

CHAPTER 6 covers fun activities that you might enjoy doing, so you can share your interests and passions with others in sign language.

In CHAPTER 7, you learn the signs for some of your favorite foods and drinks, as well as the signs for mealtimes. (Be sure to read this one with a full stomach!)

CHAPTER 8 is all about the great outdoors. You will learn signs related to nature, weather, and the four seasons.

CHAPTER 9 introduces signs for things related to school and learning, such as items you might find in your classroom and the most common school subjects.

Last but not least, in CHAPTER 10, we dive into descriptive words. Here you learn the signs for colors, shapes, sizes, and more to help you describe the world around you. And at the end of the book is a helpful RESOURCES section with my recommendations for additional tools for learning and practicing ASL.

It is a gift to teach and share this beautiful language. I am so honored to be part of your ASL learning journey. My hope is that you will continue to seek out opportunities to use your new language skills long after you finish reading this book.

Are you ready to get started? Let's go!

1

Introduction to American Sign Language

WELCOME TO CHAPTER 1! Before you start learning how to communicate with your hands, we need to go over a few things about American Sign Language (ASL) first. This chapter tells you what ASL is all about. You will also learn the manual alphabet and how to sign numbers.

WHAT IS AMERICAN SIGN LANGUAGE (ASL)?

Have you ever played charades? In this game you have to communicate ideas and words with your teammates without speaking. Isn't it amazing how much we can communicate with our bodies? ASL works just like this! It is a visual language expressed through our hands, facial expressions, and body. The main difference between charades and ASL is that ASL uses designated signs for words and ideas, as well as rule-based body language and specific movements to communicate grammar and sentence structure.

ASL began in the early 1800s at the American School for the Deaf (ASD), the first Deaf school in the United States. At the ASD they used a combination of French Sign Language, home signs (signs that developed naturally within families before there was an official sign language—back then most deaf people did not go to school and did not learn to read or write), as well as various village sign language systems from around the country. When the school opened and students from around the country came together, these different sign systems merged and ASL was born. Because ASL is a relatively new language, many signs continue to change to make ASL faster, clearer, and easier to use.

ASL is not universal. It is used in the United States as well as many parts of Canada, Africa, and much of Indonesia. Other countries have their own sign language systems. You might be surprised to know that in the United Kingdom, where English is the primary language, they use a completely different system called British Sign Language (BSL). In BSL, the signed alphabet is done with two hands, whereas in ASL it is signed with just one hand.

According to the National Association of the Deaf, there are about 48 million Deaf and hard-of-hearing (hh) people in the United States, and many of those people speak ASL. Add in all their family members, friends, teachers, and people who choose to learn ASL, and that makes for a *lot* of people speaking this language!

ASL was recognized as an official language in 1960, but it was not until the 1990s that schools started offering ASL as a foreign language option. This paved the way for more people to learn ASL and opened up more social opportunities between Deaf/hh and hearing people. Deaf people cannot learn to hear, but hearing people can learn to sign!

HOW IS ASL DIFFERENT FROM ENGLISH?

Although most languages around the world are expressed verbally, you now know there is another way we can communicate with one another: visually. Although this is the most obvious difference between ASL and English, there are other things to think of as well.

ASL's sentence structure and grammar is very different from English. Since ASL uses specific handshapes, movements, body language, and facial expressions to express context, many of the words we use to build sentences in English are not needed in ASL. Because of these differences, it is actually impossible to sign pure ASL and speak English at the same time.

Signing and speaking at the same time is called "simultaneous communication," or SimCom. When people use SimCom, English usually takes over as the dominant language and ASL becomes broken and incomplete. This can make it very difficult for a Deaf person to fully understand what is being communicated. SimCom is a great tool for individuals who have speech delays and who can still hear spoken language, but it should be avoided when communicating with the Deaf.

Signing Exact English (SEE) follows the English language exactly, whereas ASL is a completely different language with its own grammar. Although SEE is sometimes used and taught in the United States within some education systems and families, only ASL qualifies as an official language and is the one that is typically used in the Deaf community across the country. The Deaf community tends to discourage the use of SEE, as it does not represent a true language with the depth of grammar and syntax.

FINGERSPELLING BASICS

Fingerspelling in ASL uses handshapes for each letter in the English alphabet. It's mainly used for names, titles, places, and words that do not have a sign. Here are some fingerspelling tips to help you get started:

- It's easiest to use your dominant hand—the one you use to write, eat, or throw a baseball.

- Hold your hand upright, away from your body, at about shoulder height. Most of the letters are formed with your palm facing away from you.

- Try not to bounce your hand as you form the letters.

- Focus on making your handshapes clear, rather than fast.

- If you are fingerspelling more than one word, make sure to pause briefly between each word.

- When you are watching someone finger-spell a word, try to avoid saying each individual letter in your head. Instead, try to sound it out, just like you do when you read words in a book.

- When you watch someone fingerspell, look for other clues to figure out the word being spelled, such as context, the length of the word, as well as wrist movements that some letters require.

- When a word has double letters, you can either slide the letter slightly to the side or make a slight pulsing movement with that handshape to convey the repeating letter.

One fun way to practice the alphabet is to grab a buddy and play what I call the Candy Bar Game. Take turns signing every candy bar you can think of! You can also try this with other categories like colors, states, animals, or fruits and vegetables. Watch for clues to quickly figure out what your buddy is spelling.

You can also practice on your own as you go about your day. As you ride in the car or walk down the street, look around at street signs, store names, and billboards, and try to fingerspell as many of them as you can.

Don't worry about being slow at first. Fingerspelling takes practice, but the more you do it, the easier it gets!

SIGNING BASICS

In ASL, each sign represents a specific word or idea. Sometimes a sign represents an exact English word. But some English words have multiple meanings, and so will have multiple signs. Take, for instance, the English word "run." We can *run* for president, *run* a race, or *run* out of milk. It's the same word in English, but each use represents a different concept, so there are several different signs for **RUN** in ASL. If we signed the wrong one, it might look like we are saying, "milk is running away!" Think also of the English word "get." We can go *get* our backpack, we can *get* sick, or we can *get* up in the morning. **GET** also has multiple signs.

Handshape

Each sign uses a specific handshape. Sometimes a sign is done on the same location of the body with the same movement but the handshape is different, which means it represents a different word. For example, the sign for **PINK** is done with the "P" handshape on the chin, whereas the sign for **RED** is exactly the same but you use your index finger instead of the "P" handshape.

Location

Each sign is made at a specific location on the body or within your signing space. You will learn that the signs for **MOM** and

DAD are the exact same handshape, but each sign is done at a different location on the body to show whether you are referring to the male (dad) or female (mom).

Movement

In addition to handshape and location, each sign has a special movement. Some signs might use tapping, whereas others might use a circular movement or rocking motion. The signs for **MOM** and **GRANDMA** have the same handshape *and* the same location, but each utilizes a specific movement to specify the word. (The sign for **MOM** is a tap on the chin, whereas the movement for **GRANDMA** arches outward away from the chin.)

Orientation

Orientation refers to the direction your palm faces when you make a sign. For some signs, your palm faces away from you, and for others it faces toward you, downward, or to the side. When you learn the signs for **KNOW** and **DON'T KNOW**, you will notice that when you sign **DON'T KNOW**, your palm shifts away from your body during the sign. This is the same for **LIKE** and **DON'T LIKE**, and **WANT** and **DON'T WANT**.

Facial expression

Facial expression is a very important part of ASL and, believe it or not, is necessary to express grammar, emotion, and other language information. Some signs may use exactly the same handshape, location, movement, and orientation, except the head shakes to show negation (no) or nods to show affirmation (yes). Take for example the signs for **UNDERSTAND** and **DON'T UNDERSTAND**. The only difference between these signs is the head nodding or shaking to show that you do understand or you do not understand. You will also learn that you can use facial expression to convey words like "very." When you are signing the word **EXCITED**, if you want to say *very* **EXCITED** you would make an even more excited expression.

HOW TO READ THE SIGNS IN THIS BOOK

As you use the sign illustrations in this book, keep in mind that all signs are drawn from the signer's perspective. All of the models are right-handed, so if you are right-handed you will be copying the signs in reverse. Picture yourself in the same position as the model as you practice the signs. If you are left-handed, then you will follow the signs as if you are looking at yourself in the mirror. In signs with hands outlined in black and in red, the black hand notes where you start the sign movement, and the red hand shows where you end the movement. The arrows show the direction of the sign movement. The sign descriptions often use a letter handshape such as "B handshape" or "O handshape." This means that you will make the handshape of that letter from the manual alphabet to form the sign. If you forget a letter handshape, you can always go back to the alphabet section (page 7) to refresh your memory!

ALPHABET

There are four letters in the alphabet that are not signed with the palm facing outward. **G** and **H** are signed with the fingers pointed to the side and the palm facing the body. **P** and **Q** are signed with both the fingers and palm down. The rest of the letters are all signed with your palm facing the person you are signing with, but with your hand a slight angle, which is more comfortable for the wrist. Take care not to strain your wrist by keeping your hand facing directly forward.

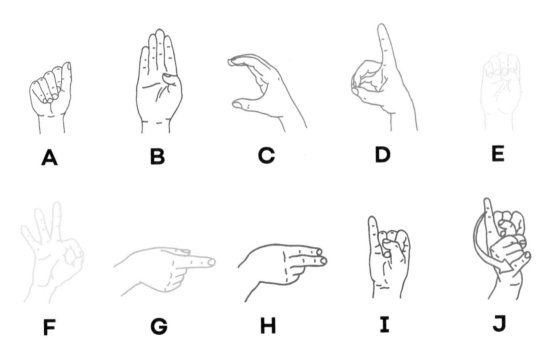

A   B   C   D   E

F   G   H   I   J

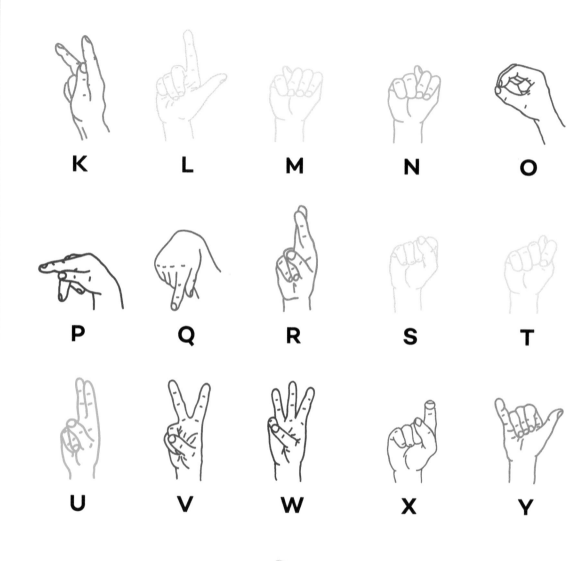

K   L   M   N   O

P   Q   R   S   T

U   V   W   X   Y

Z

NUMBERS

ASL numbers are all done with one hand. It's a very convenient way to count, as you'll soon see. Numbers 1 through 5 and 11 through 15 are signed with the palm facing your body. The rest of the numbers are signed with the palm facing away from the body. When numbers 1 through 5 are done in combination with other numbers, such as 43 or 58, they are signed with your palm forward, rather than facing your body.

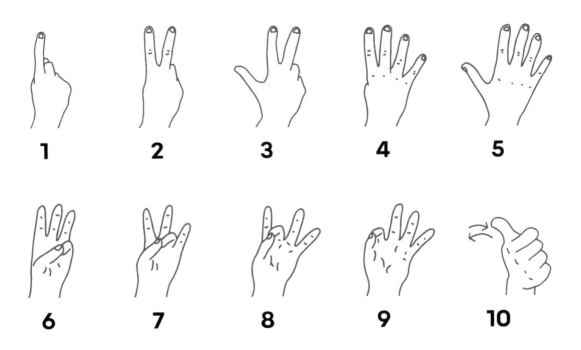

1	**2**	**3**	**4**	**5**
6	**7**	**8**	**9**	**10**

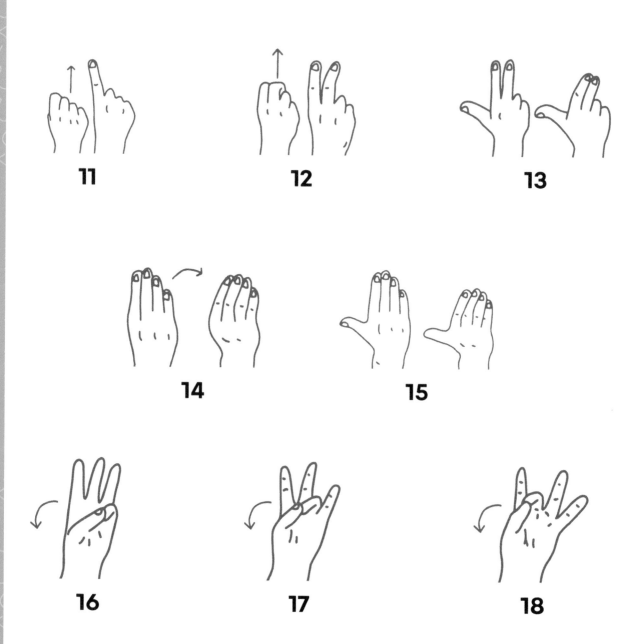

11

12

13

14

15

16

17

18

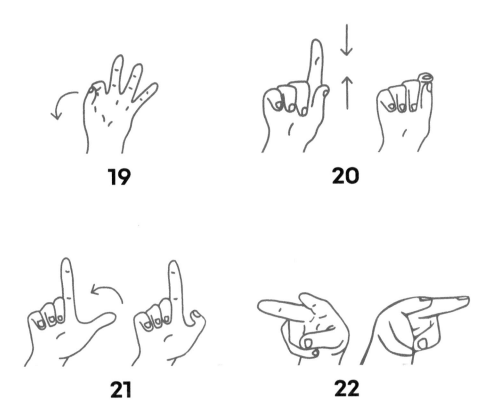

19

20

21

22

23

24

25

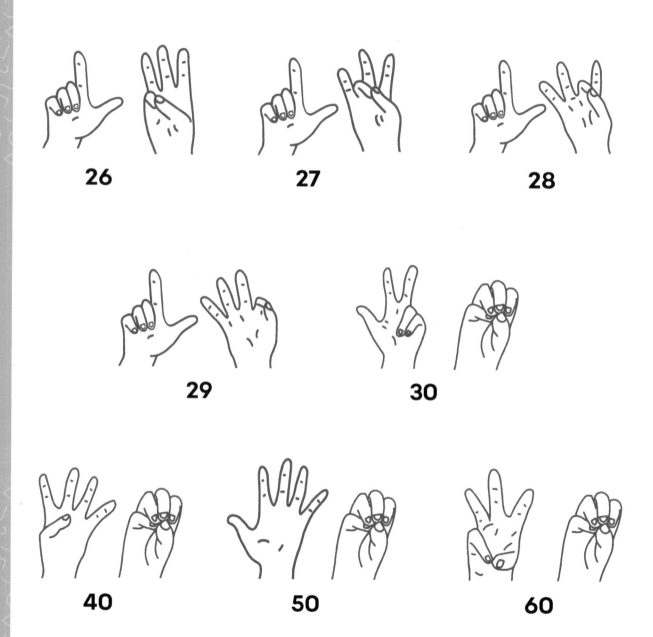

26

27

28

29

30

40

50

60

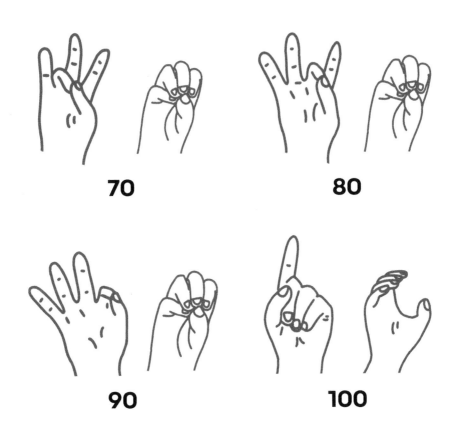

70

80

90

100

2

Conversation Basics

LET'S DIVE INTO some general conversation starters and common phrases you might use when you first meet someone—things like "hello," "please," "thank you," and how to introduce yourself. We'll also go over how to ask questions in American Sign Language (ASL), including the facial expressions to use. Are you ready to get started? Me too!

Hello

With your palm facing out, place a flat hand at the side of your forehead. Then pull your hand away from your head, almost like you are saluting someone.

My name is

Put your flat hand on your chest to sign **MY**. Then, with two hands and keeping your palms facing inward, make an "H" handshape (see page 7) on both hands, then cross the top fingers over the bottom fingers and tap down two times to sign **NAME**.

What's your name?

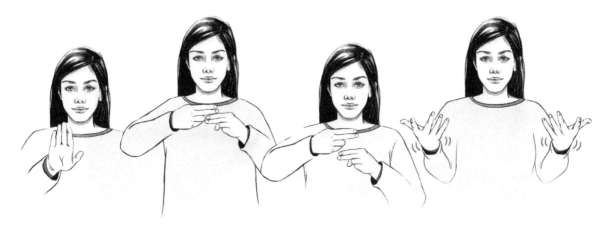

With your palm facing out, put your flat hand forward to sign **YOUR**. Then make an "H" handshape (see page 7) on each hand and tap your top fingers onto your bottom fingers two times to sign **NAME**. Last, make the sign for **WHAT** by holding out both hands open with your palms up and moving them side to side.

Nice to meet you

Start this phrase by making the sign for
NICE: with one palm facing down and
your other palm facing up, cross the
hand with the palm facing down over
your other palm. To sign **MEET**, with
your index fingers both pointing up and
palms facing each other, close your
hands and bring them together until
your fists touch. Last, sign **YOU** by
pointing your index finger at the person
you are meeting!

Please

Place a flat palm on your chest and make small circles around your heart as if you are gently rubbing it.

Me/I

Using your index finger, point to the middle of your chest like you are pointing at yourself.

Sorry

This sign is similar to the sign for **PLEASE**, but you make your hand into a fist and then move it in circular motions around your heart.

Thank you/ you're welcome

With your palm facing in, make a flat handshape and touch your fingers to your mouth or chin area. Then bring your hand out toward the person to whom you are saying "thank you." The sign for **YOU'RE WELCOME** is the same as for **THANK YOU**!

Excuse me

Hold your hands in front of you, bottom palm facing up and top palm facing down. Brush the tips of your fingers on the top hand across the tips of your fingers on your bottom hand as if you are wiping something off of your fingertips.

I love you

With your palm facing out, put up your pinkie, index finger, and thumb, and fold down the other two fingers. You can remember this one by imagining your pinkie as the "I" and your index finger and thumb making the "L" in love, and the "U" shape in the middle for "you." You can even wave this handshape to say, "Bye, I love you!"

Deaf/hard-of-hearing (hh) people can have service dogs, too! Service dogs can be trained to alert deaf/hh people of important sounds and notifications in their environment, such as a knock at the door or the phone ringing.

Maybe

Make a flat handshape with both hands, palms facing up. Then move your hands up and down alternately, as if your hands are scales weighing whether you want something or not.

Yes

With your palm facing out, make a fist and bend it down and up from the wrist. To remember this sign, think of a head nodding up and down!

No

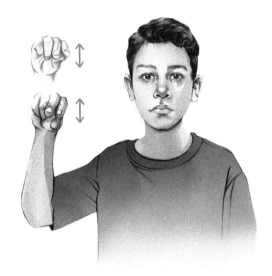

With your palm facing out, make a "3" handshape (see page 9), keeping your fingers close together; open and close your fingers a few times. If you want to make a firm expression of "no," only open and close your fingers one time.

Who

With your palm facing to the side, place your thumb on your chin and point your index finger. Bend your index finger repeatedly up and down. To remember the sign, think of the beak of an owl when it hoots "hoo, hoo!"

What

Hold your hands in front of you with your palms facing up and move them side to side in opposite directions a few times, as if you are gesturing "huh?"

When

Bring the tips of your index fingers together, and then use one index finger to draw a little circle around the other fingertip. Imagine you're drawing the shape of a little round clock.

? DID YOU KNOW

In American Sign Language, there are certain facial expressions you make when asking questions. To make a yes or no expression, you arch your eyebrows up and lean your head forward. To make a "wh" question (who, what, when, where, why, how, which), you furrow your eyebrows and tilt your head to the side.

Where

With your palm facing out, point your index finger and wave it back and forth. This sign reminds me of a dog's tail wagging back and forth. You can think, *Where's the dog?* as you wag your finger.

Why

Place your open hand next to your forehead with the palm facing in and wiggle your middle finger up and down a couple of times. You will almost be scratching your head, but not quite.

How

With both palms facing in and your hands in a loose fist shape, bring your knuckles together. Twist both hands forward until your palms are slightly facing up.

Which

With your palms facing inward, away from your body, make an "A" handshape (see page 7) with each hand. Then move your hands up and down alternately, as if they are scales weighing which thing you want the most!

From

With both hands in the "1" handshape (see page 9), point one index finger toward the other, then bend that finger into a hook shape as you move it back toward your body.

Here

Place both hands in a flat handshape in front of you, palms facing up. Then move them both in circular motions away from each other.

Deaf culture etiquette

Now that you know some basics, you can start communicating with people who use American Sign Language! Here are some important tips for interacting with deaf and hard-of-hearing (hh) people.

- Remember that not all deaf/hh people use sign language to communicate. Just because you see someone wearing hearing aids or cochlear implants doesn't mean they know or use sign language. If you would like to start up a conversation with them, it is polite to first ask if they use sign language to communicate or if they prefer to read lips.

- If a deaf/hh person prefers to read lips, be careful not to overenunciate or move your mouth in exaggerated speech movements, as this can actually make it harder to understand you. Make sure that your mouth is clearly visible and not covered by hair, food, clothing, paper, your hands, or your favorite furry critter!

- Do not raise your voice or speak extremely slowly. The best way to speak is at a slightly slower speed with clear mouth movements and a normal volume. Eye contact is very important. Always make sure you are facing the person with whom you are communicating.

- Be patient and don't give up! Use a piece of paper and pen, text messages on your phone, or gestures to help get your message across.

- Some deaf/hh people wear hearing aids or cochlear implants and some do not. It is best not to judge or question people's choice regarding this, and always be respectful.

3

Home, Family, and Pets

WELCOME TO CHAPTER 3! In this chapter you'll learn signs for family members, rooms in your home, and common pets. You will notice that all male signs are made from the top part of your face and all female signs are made from the bottom part of your face. A great way to practice the signs in this chapter is to walk around your house and make the signs for any rooms you pass through, any family members you see, and any pets that are snuggled up in your home (or pets you would like to have!).

Many Deaf/hard-of-hearing people have special lights in their homes to signal when the doorbell or phone rings, or when the fire alarm goes off.

Home

Close all of your fingertips together into a handshape that looks like a flat "O." Touch your fingertips to your face next your mouth (where you eat) and then bring them up toward your cheek (where you lay your head to sleep).

Bedroom

Start this sign by making the sign for
BED: place your flat handshape
against your cheek like you are laying
your head down on your bed. To sign
ROOM, place both hands in a flat
handshape in front of you, palms facing
each other like two walls of a room.
Then shift the hand positions to make
the other two walls with both palms
facing toward your body.

Living room

Start by making the sign for **LIVE** or **LIFE**. With both hands at the bottom of your chest next to your body, make two "A" handshapes (see page 7) and then move both hands up your chest toward your shoulders. To sign

ROOM, place both hands flat in front of you, palms facing each other like two walls of a room. Then shift the hand positions to make the other two walls with both palms facing toward your body.

Bathroom

With your palm facing out, make a "T" handshape (see page 8) and shake the "T" handshape side to side. You can increase the intensity of this sign by making the movements more swift and urgent, depending on how badly you need to use the bathroom!

Kitchen

Place one hand flat in front of you, palm facing up. Then put your other hand above it in a "K" handshape (see page 8). Place your "K" hand, palm-side down, on top of your upturned palm. Then flip your "K" hand over as if you are flipping a pancake.

? DID YOU KNOW

When Deaf people go to one another's homes, they are known to gather in the kitchen to visit. This is most likely because the lighting is usually the best in the kitchen so they can see one another well as they converse.

TV

With your palm facing out, sign the handshapes for the letters "T" and "V" (see page 8).

Computer

Make a "C" handshape (see page 7) with one hand and bend your other arm in front of you. Make circular motions with the "C" on your other arm. To remember the sign, think of a gear turning in circles.

Phone

Make a "Y" handshape (see page 8) and tap it to your cheek as if you are holding a phone up to your mouth and ear.

Mom

Make a "5" handshape (see page 9) and touch your thumb to the lower part of your face. Remember, all female signs are made on the lower part of the face.

Dad

Use the same "5" handshape that you used for **MOM**, but now make it at the top of your head with your thumb touching your forehead. Remember, all male signs are made on the upper part of your face.

Brother

Start with a closed fist up toward the top of your head to refer to the male part of the face. Place your other hand out in front of you in a fist as well. As you bring your top hand down, stick out your index fingers on both hands and then have the top fist land on the bottom fist.

Sister

Start with a closed fist touching the bottom part of your face by your chin to refer to the female part of the face. Place your other hand out in front of you in a fist as well. As you bring your top hand down, stick out your index fingers on both hands and have the top fist land on the bottom fist.

Son/daughter

Baby

Using a flat handshape, start by referring to the male or female part of the face. For **SON**, start with your hand at your forehead, as pictured above. For **DAUGHTER**, start with your hand near your mouth. Then bring your hand down to your other arm like you are holding a baby. (You do not need to make the rocking motions like you do for the **BABY** sign.)

Cradle your arms down in front of your stomach and rock them side to side, the way you would gently rock a baby.

Grandma

Start by making the sign for **MOM** (page 38) on the lower part of your face, then bring your open hand forward in an arching movement.

Grandpa

Start by making the sign for **DAD** (page 38) on the upper part of your face, then bring your open hand forward in an arching movement.

Aunt/uncle

Cousin

For **AUNT**, make an "A" handshape
(see page 7) next to the lower (female)
part of the face and wiggle your fist in a
slight circular or twisting motion. You
can make the sign for **UNCLE** the
exact same way, except with a
"U" handshape next to the top (male)
part of your face.

Make a "C" handshape (see page 7) on
the side of your face in the middle and
wiggle your hand. This sign is done in
the middle of the face because a cousin
can be male or a female. To be specific
about a female cousin or a male cousin,
make this sign on the lower or upper
part of the face, respectively.

Pet

Make one hand into a fist, palm facing down. Then use your top hand to make a petting motion on your fist, like you are petting an animal. Short, quick movements sign the noun **PET**, whereas longer, more drawn-out motions sign the verb **PET**.

Cat

Make an "F" handshape (see page 7) on your cheek and pull it out to the side away from your face. A helpful way to remember this sign is to think of the "F" handshape as whiskers on a cat!

Dog

Place one hand in front of your body and make a snapping motion with your fingers. A good way to remember this sign is to think of how people often snap their fingers to call their dog.

Fish

With one hand in a flat handshape and your palm facing to the side, wiggle your hand in and out like a fish swimming through the water.

? DID YOU KNOW

Instead of clapping at performances and events, Deaf people applaud by shaking their hands in the air to visually show performers or speakers that they did a great job.

? DID YOU KNOW

Some people sign in their sleep just like some people talk in their sleep. Now that you are learning American Sign Language, maybe you will, too!

Bird

In front of your mouth, bring your index finger and thumb together repeatedly to look like a bird's beak opening and closing as it chirps.

What's the difference between Deaf and deaf?

If you've ever read a book or article about Deaf people, you might have noticed that sometimes the word "deaf" is spelled with a capital "D" and sometimes with a lowercase "d." Writers often use a capital "D" when referring to people who identify as culturally Deaf, meaning they use American Sign Language (ASL) and are actively involved in the Deaf community. When deaf is used with a lowercase "d," it simply indicates an inability to hear. People who lose their hearing later in life and do not learn ASL are generally referred to with a lowercase "d." Most people who identify as capital "D" Deaf are proud of their Deafness and their Deaf heritage.

That said, you do not have to have a certain level of hearing loss or speech ability/inability to identify as Deaf with a capital D. It's all about how a person chooses to identify. For instance, someone who is hard-of-hearing can refer to themselves as Deaf with a capital "D" if they use ASL and identify with the Deaf community and culture.

Not all deaf people become part of the Deaf community or learn ASL. Some are raised focusing on developing speech and lipreading abilities in order to interact with the hearing world. This is a personal decision, and you should never judge someone based on how they choose to identify.

4

Action Words

WELCOME TO CHAPTER 4, where you'll learn important signs for building sentences, as well as some action words and directional verbs. These new signs will help you communicate what you're doing or want to do. You will also learn signs that help you ask questions and give commands, and the different ways to express negation in ASL. Let's go!

Go

With your palms facing out, stick up both index fingers and move them forward at the same time, as if indicating something moving away from you.

Come

This is signed just like **GO**, with both index fingers up, but this time with your palms facing in toward your body. Move both index fingers toward your body at the same time, as if indicating something coming closer to you.

Want

Put both hands out in front of you, palms facing up. Bend the knuckles of your fingers into a claw handshape and pull your hands toward your body, as if you are pulling in something that you want.

Don't want

This is signed almost like the sign for **WANT**, with both hands in a claw handshape. But instead of pulling your hands in toward you, you start with your palms facing toward you and then turn your palms away from your body and move your hands down, as if you are pushing away something you don't want.

? DID YOU KNOW

You can show intensity in American Sign Language by making your movements more urgent or drawn out. For instance, when you make the sign for NEED (page 62), think about how badly you need something. If you *really* need something, sign with more intensity. If you only *slightly* need something, sign with less urgent movements.

Like

Start with your hand in a "5" hand-shape (see page 9), palm facing in, then bring your thumb and middle finger together, as if you are pulling on a string attached to your heart.

Don't like

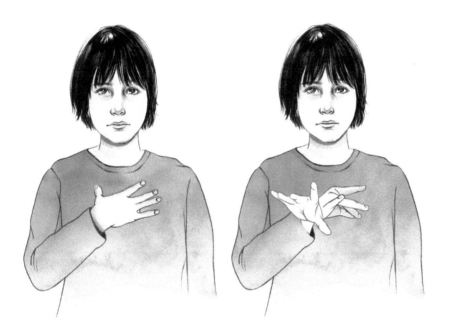

This sign is almost like the sign for **LIKE**. Start with your hand in a "5" handshape (see page 9), palm facing in, then bring your thumb and middle finger together as if you are pulling on a string attached to your heart. Instead of pulling on the string, reverse the sign away from your chest, as if you're picking something off your shirt and flicking it away.

Know

Bring all of your fingers together into a flat handshape and bend the hand slightly. Touch your fingertips to your forehead. Sometimes people tap their head a few times, or you can just tap once. To remember the sign, think of how when you know something, it's in your head.

Don't know

This one is almost like the sign for **KNOW**, but after you touch your forehead with your fingertips, twist your palm out, away from your body. To remember this sign, think of how when you don't know something, it is not in your head.

Practice

Run

Point to the side with your non-dominant hand, palm facing toward your body. With your dominant hand, make an "A" handshape (see page 7) and rub it back and forth across your other index finger as if you are polishing it. To remember the sign, think of how you "polish" a skill by practicing it.

With your palms facing together, make an "L" handshape (see page 8) with both hands. Wrap the index finger of one hand around the thumb of the other hand. Wiggle the index finger of the front hand as you move both of your hands forward.

? DID YOU KNOW

In American Sign Language, negatives are usually at the end of a sentence. Some ways to show negation are by shaking your head **(DON'T UNDERSTAND, DON'T HAVE)** or pushing a sign away from you **(DON'T WANT, DON'T LIKE)**.

Have/don't have

Make flat handshapes with both hands, palms facing in toward the body. Bend them slightly at the bottom knuckle and touch the tips of your fingers of both hands on your upper chest, just inside your shoulders. To sign that you **DON'T HAVE** something, shake your head side to side while making this sign.

Understand/
don't understand

Misunderstand

With your palm facing in, make a fist and hold it up to the side of your forehead, then flick your index finger upward. To remember the sign, think of a lightbulb turning on in your head. To sign that you **DON'T UNDERSTAND**, do this sign while shaking your head side to side.

Make a "K" handshape (see page 8) and touch your forehead with your index finger, then rotate your hand to touch your forehead with your middle finger. To remember the sign, think about how when you realize you don't actually understand something, your brain does a little flip!

Say/tell

With your palm facing in, touch your index finger to your mouth or chin. Then move your hand away from your body, keeping your palm facing in. To remember the sign, think of a word coming out of your mouth.

Talk

With your palm facing to the side, make a "4" handshape (see page 9). Tap your index finger against your mouth or chin a few times. To remember the sign, think of lots of words coming out of your mouth.

Think

Touch your index finger to your forehead as if pointing to a thought that's in your head.

Guess/miss

Create a "C" handshape (see page 7) near the side of your face and move your hand across the front of your face and close your hand into a fist. This is also the sign for **MISS**, as in "I missed the bus" (but not the same sign for when you're missing something or someone, like a friend who's moved away).

Can/could/able/possible

With your palms facing out, make your fists into either an "A" or "S" handshape (see pages 7–8)—the location of your thumb isn't incredibly important—then drop both fists down at the wrists. Repeat this movement to sign **ABLE** or **POSSIBLE**.

Can't

With your palms facing down, make fists and then stick out both index fingers, with one hovering above the other. Bring your top finger down and knock your other finger as you pass by it. To remember the sign, think of a child reaching to touch something hot and their parent knocking their finger out of the way so they don't get burned.

Stop

Hold out one hand in a flat handshape with your palm facing up, then drop the other flat hand, palm facing to the side, onto your bottom palm as if you are chopping something in half.

Ask

Place both hands in flat handshapes with your palms facing each other. Rotate your hands up and bring your palms together until they touch. The final position of the sign looks like your hands are in prayer.

Need/must/should/have to

Make an "X" handshape (see page 8) with one hand like a hook and pull your whole hand as if you are pulling down on a cord. This is also the sign for **MUST**, **SHOULD**, and **HAVE TO**.

Help/Can I help you?/Can you help me?

Hold out one hand in a flat handshape, palm facing up, in front of your body. With your other hand in an "A" handshape (see page 7), set it on the palm of your other hand. This is also a directional verb, so if you move this sign toward someone with a questioning look on your face, you are signing "**CAN I HELP YOU?**" If you move the sign toward you with a questioning look, you are signing, **CAN YOU HELP ME?**

Technology for the Deaf

Life for a deaf or hard-of-hearing (hh) person today is easier in many ways than it was in the past. For one thing, closed captioning became available in 1973, which allows viewers to read the dialogue at the bottom of the screen. Before then, there was no way for deaf/hh people to understand what was being said on TV without having an interpreter. Now many movie theaters offer personal closed captioning devices for deaf/hh people, which has made going to the movies much easier for people with hearing loss.

Because deaf people cannot hear on the phone, for a long time they had to rely on family members and friends to make phone calls for them. For many years, deaf people used a big clunky device called a TTY/TDD to make phone calls. It looked and functioned like an old-fashioned typewriter and allowed people to send typed messages back and forth! But today deaf people can use texting, online chatting, and video calling on smart phones or computers to communicate. There are also videophones, which allow a Deaf person to sign directly to another Deaf person.

If a Deaf person wants to call a hearing person, they use what is called the Video Relay Service (VRS). With VRS, a person first connects with a sign language interpreter, then with the hearing person they're calling. The interpreter translates the messages back and forth. We also now have CaptionCall phones that provide nearly instant captions on a phone call. All of this new technology has made it much easier for deaf/hh people to stay connected to their family, friends, and community!

5

Thoughts and Feelings

CHAPTER 5 IS ALL about signs related to thoughts and feelings. These signs are fun because they use a lot of different facial expressions! As you now know, facial expression is a very big part of American Sign Language (ASL), and this is especially true when it comes to communicating feelings. You can also express sarcasm in ASL by making a facial expression that doesn't match the feeling you're signing. For example, if you sign "I love school" with a happy face, you truly mean that you love school. But if you sign, "I love school" with an annoyed face, you are being sarcastic and saying that you don't *really* love school (*eye roll*).

DID YOU KNOW

Facial expression is especially helpful in communicating degrees of emotion. The difference between the words *tired* and *exhausted*, or *excited* and *thrilled*, are shown by an exaggerated facial expression and increased movement intensity.

Happy

With your palm flat on your chest, bring your hand upward repeatedly while smiling and making a happy expression on your face.

Excited/What's up?/thrilled

Fine

With your palms facing toward your body, make a "5" handshape (see page 9) with your middle fingers bent in. Then, with a joyful expression on your face, make alternating inward circular motions with your hands, tapping your middle fingers to your chest as you go. If you change this sign so your hands move upward at the same time, it becomes the sign for **WHAT'S UP?** or **THRILLED**.

With your palm facing to the side, make a "5" handshape (see page 9) and tap your thumb to your chest a few times.

Hurt/headache/ stomachache

With your palms facing in, place your hands in front of your chest and point your index fingers at each other. Then twist your hands in opposite directions from the wrist. This is a locational sign, so if you wanted to show a **HEADACHE**, you would sign it up near your head, and for a **STOMACHACHE**, down in front of your stomach.

Sad

With your palms facing in, make a "5" handshape (see page 9) on each side of your face. Pull your hands downward as if your face is drooping with sadness. Be sure to make a sad facial expression as you do this sign.

Frustrated

With your palm facing out, make a flat closed-fingered handshape in front of your chin. Bring your hand back to tap the back of your fingers against your chin a few times. Show a look of frustration as you do this sign.

Scared

Starting with your fists in front of your chest, palms facing in, quickly open your hands into the "5" handshape (see page 9) with a frightened look on your face.

Jealous

With your palm facing to the side, make an "X" handshape (see page 8). Touch your index finger to your cheek and then twist your palm toward you, keeping the "X" handshape, while making an envious expression.

Angry/grumpy

With your palm facing in, make a "5" handshape (see page 9) in front of your face and close your fingers abruptly into a claw. If you repeat this movement, it becomes the sign for **GRUMPY**. Make sure you have a mad face when you do this sign!

Bored

With your palm facing out and hand in the "1" handshape, touch it against the side of your nose. Rotate your hand so your palm ends up facing you. Make a bored and uninterested look as you do this sign.

Curious

With one hand, make an "F" hand-shape (see page 7). Pinch a little bit of the skin on the front of your neck and wiggle your hand. Make an expression of curiosity as you do this sign.

Embarrassed

Proud

With your palms facing in, make a "5" handshape (see page 9) on either side of your face. Move your hands alternately in an upward circular motion, as if you were flushing from embarrassment. Make an embarrassed facial expression.

With your palm facing down, make an "A" handshape (see page 7). Touch the tip of your thumb to the bottom of your chest and pull your hand up in a straight line, as if you were zipping up a uniform you're proud to wear. Make a proud expression on your face as you do this sign.

Tired

With your palms facing toward each other in front of your shoulders, make a "5" handshape (see page 9), with both hands bent down at the wrist. Curl both hands down, rotating toward your body at the wrist, until your palms face away from each other, as if your body is slumping from exhaustion. Show a tired look on your face.

? DID YOU KNOW

Sometimes there is more than one sign for a word. You may look in two different American Sign Language dictionaries and find completely different signs for the same word. This is usually due to some language variations in different regions of the country—just as we find in English.

Surprised

With both hands in fists, pinch your thumbs and index fingers together next to your eyes. Then open the two fingers suddenly as if you saw something surprising. Show a look of surprise on your face.

Silly

With your palm facing to the side, make a "Y" handshape (see page 8). Touch your thumb to your nose and move your hand side to side with a silly or joking look on your face.

Lonely

Touch your index finger to your chin and move it in a downward circular motion a few times. Make a sad facial expression as you do this sign.

Feel/sensitive

With your palm facing in, make a "5" handshape (see page 9) and tilt your middle finger in until it touches your chest. Bring your hand up repeatedly, as if you were stroking your heart. If you make this sign in a downward motion, it becomes the sign for **SENSITIVE**.

Laugh/smile

Cry

Touch the sides of your mouth with your index fingers and stroke them outward repeatedly as if drawing a happy face. If you do this sign with just one movement, it is the sign for **SMILE**. Make sure to smile big as you do this sign!

With the other fingers in a fist, touch your index fingers to your cheeks below your eyes, and move them downward repeatedly, as if tears are streaming down your cheeks. Make a sad face as you do this sign.

What is an interpreter?

Have you ever seen a sign language interpreter at your school or an event? This person is trained to translate spoken language into visual language. Interpreters are critical to the Deaf community, because they help make information and experiences accessible to those who cannot hear.

A sign language interpreter must know more than the basic signs. They must have a strong vocabulary, a deep understanding of grammar, and be able to accurately convey feelings, context, and subtext of words.

Being an interpreter is an important job that provides access to the Deaf community. We need interpreters in schools, businesses, Video Relay Service companies, medical facilities, court-rooms, community events, conferences, the theater, and much more. Many colleges offer training programs for interpreters. With enough practice and training, even you can become an interpreter!

6

Fun Activities

YOU ARE GOING to love this chapter because it's all about sports, hobbies, and fun activities! With these signs, you'll be able to use American Sign Language (ASL) to communicate some of the things that you love to do. To practice these signs on your own, imagine yourself talking to a Deaf person about your favorite activities inside and outside of school.

Sports/athletics/ competition/race

With your palms facing each other, make an "A" handshape (see page 7) with both hands. Then brush your knuckles back and forth against each other a few times. This is also the sign for **ATHLETICS**, **COMPETITION**, and **RACE!**

Soccer/kick

With your palms facing in toward your body and fingers pointing sideways, make a flat handshape with one hand and a loose fist with the other. Hold the hand in a loose fist out in front of your body and bring your other hand up to knock the bottom of that hand several times, as if you are "kicking" it. If you do this sign once, it is the sign for **KICK**.

Baseball

Hold your closed fists together, one above the other, as if you are holding a baseball bat, and make a couple of small swinging motions.

Basketball

Football

There are several ways to sign **BASKETBALL**. The most common way is to make a "3" handshape (see page 9) on both hands, palms facing each other, and rock your hands back and forth. Imagine you are holding a basketball and getting ready to toss it!

Make a "5" handshape (see page 9) on both hands, palms facing each other, and bring your hands together to interlock your fingers, almost like players tackling each other. Repeat this movement twice.

Play

With palms facing in, make a "Y" hand-shape (see page 8) with both hands. Then twist your wrists outward and inward at least two times. This is the sign for the verb **PLAY**. If you want to say, "I am going to act in a **PLAY**," you would use a different sign (see **THEATER**, page 90).

Team/family/class

With your palms facing out, make a "T" handshape (see page 8) with both hands. Touch your index fingers together and then rotate them away from you until your pinkie fingers meet and your palms are facing toward you. If you want to sign **FAMILY**, make this sign with "F" handshapes (see page 7). If you make the sign with "C" hand-shapes, it becomes the sign for **CLASS**.

Win

Make a fist with one hand. Make your other hand into a "C" handshape (see page 7) and close it into a fist as you brush across the top of the other fist. To remember the sign, imagine someone else is holding a trophy and you reach over to grab it!

Lose

Hold one hand out in a flat handshape with your palm facing up. Make a "V" handshape (see page 8) with your other hand, and slap it across your flat palm—almost like someone doing a belly flop! Note that this is the sign for when you lose a game or a match, but not the sign for when you lose something, like a pen.

Game

With your palms facing in, make "A" handshapes (see page 7) with both hands and gently bang your knuckles against each other repeatedly.

Walking

With your palms facing down, make flat or slightly bent handshapes with both hands. Alternately move your hands back and forth, like feet walking on the ground.

Bicycle/biking

Hold both hands out in front of you as if you are holding the handlebars of a bike. Then make alternating circular motions with your fists to mimic the motion of pedaling a bicycle.

Dance

Place one hand in a flat handshape in front of your body with your palm facing up. Make a "V" handshape (see page 8) with your other hand, pointing your fingertips down to the flat hand. Sweep your "V" hand back and forth along your flat hand, like legs across a dance floor.

Art/drawing

Place one hand in a flat handshape in front of your body, palm facing up. Make an "I" handshape (see page 7) with your other hand and touch your pinkie to your flat hand. Then "draw" an imaginary squiggly line down your palm, just like you're drawing with a pen on paper.

Paint

Make a flat handshape with one hand, palm facing to the side and fingers pointing up. Then make a flat hand-shape with your other hand, palm facing down, and brush your fingertips up and down the vertical hand, as if you're painting at an easel with a paintbrush.

Music

Make both hands into flat handshapes. Hold one hand in front of your body, palm facing up. Swing your other hand, palm facing to the side, back and forth above your bottom arm.

Photography

Make both hands into an "L" handshape (see page 8) and hold them on either side of your forehead. With your dominant hand, wiggle your index finger up and down as if you are snapping pictures.

Travel/trip

With your palm facing down, make a bent "V" handshape (see page 8), which resembles the front wheels of a car. Move the hand away from your body, as if you are moving a car forward to go on a trip. This is also the sign for **TRIP**.

? DID YOU KNOW

Many Deaf/hard-of-hearing people love music! It's not uncommon to find them gathered around speakers with the volume and bass turned up high so they can feel the vibrations.

Theater/play/ perform/drama

With your palms facing each other, make an "A" handshape (see page 7) with both hands. Then touch the tips of your thumbs against your chest and move them in alternating downward circles. This is also the sign for **PLAY** (noun), **PERFORM**, and **DRAMA**.

Movie

Make both hands into a "5" handshape (see page 9). Touch your palms together with the fingers of one hand pointing in a relaxed sideways position and the fingers of the other hand pointing up. Rock or slide the hand with your fingers facing up against your other palm in a repeated motion. To remember the sign, imagine those old movie reels spinning film through projectors.

Choosing your sign name

At birth, we are given a name that can be expressed in both verbal and written language. In American Sign Language, visual names are also given to Deaf people as well as their family members, friends, teachers, interpreters, and others so they can be identified with a sign. Although some people may make up their own name sign, it is a sign of respect and approval by the Deaf community if a Deaf person gives you your name sign. If someone does not have a name sign, their name can be signed by fingerspelling the corresponding letters in the alphabet.

There are lots of different ways to come up with a name sign. Some are made using the first letter of a person's English name, and some use a person's initials, such as "T.J." Others use a handshape that's not at all related to the person's English name, but instead represents something related to their personality, physical traits, interests, or skills. Some name signs are based on something unique or memorable that someone did as an infant or child, such as a baby who was extremely energetic and always tried to escape their crib.

If you have a Deaf friend or family member, ask them if they will help you come up with a name sign that feels just right for YOU!

7

Food and Drink

WARNING: AVOID READING this chapter on an empty stomach! Otherwise, you'll get hungry as you learn the signs for foods like **HAMBURGER** and **ICE CREAM**. One of the very first signs I learned was **PIZZA**, and to this day it remains my favorite! We will also go over the signs for mealtimes and needs like **THIRSTY** and **HUNGRY**. To practice these signs, look at your plate at every meal and see if you know the signs for some of the food you're eating. Ready? Let's take a bite.

Hungry

With your palm facing in, make a "C" handshape (page 7) at the top of your chest and drag it down to your stomach. If you want to show that you are *very* hungry, sign the word slowly.

Full

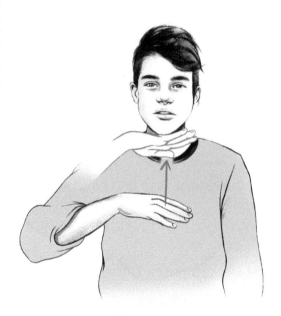

With your palm facing down, make a flat handshape in front of your chest. Then bring your hand up to hit the bottom of your chin—as if you ate so much food, it filled you up all the way to the top of your throat!

Thirsty

With your palm facing in, point your index finger up and draw a line down your throat as if you're showing that your throat is dry and you need a drink.

Food/eat

Hold your hand in front of your mouth and touch all of your fingers together as if you are holding a piece of food. Then touch your fingertips to your mouth like you're putting the food in your mouth. This is also the sign for **EAT**.

Drink

Make a "C" handshape (see page 7), like you are holding a cup. Then bring your hand up to your mouth like you're tilting the cup to take a drink.

Breakfast/ lunch/dinner

With your palm facing to the side, make a "B" handshape (see page 7) and hold your hand up to your mouth. Then gently tap your fingers to your mouth as you make a circular motion. If you change your handshape to "L," this becomes the sign for **LUNCH**, and if you change it to "D" it becomes **DINNER**.

Pizza

With your palm facing up, bring your fingertips toward your mouth as if you're holding a slice of pizza and about to take a big bite!

One advantage of knowing sign language is you can talk with your mouth full! It is quite difficult, though, to sign with your hands full.

Fruit

With your palm facing in, make an "F" handshape (page 7). Touch your pinched thumb and index finger to your cheek and then twist them back and forth like you are making a dimple in your cheek.

Vegetables

Make a "V" handshape (see page 8). Touch your index finger to your cheek and twist your hand back and forth.

Cookie

Hold out your hand in a flat handshape with your palm facing up. With your other hand, make a claw handshape and touch your fingertips to your palm, then twist your wrist and touch down on your palm again as if you are cutting cookie dough with a cookie cutter.

Cheese

Place your hands horizontally in front of you with your palms facing toward each other. Make a "5" handshape (see page 9) with each hand and then press your top palm to your bottom palm. Twist your top palm a couple of times as if you're pressing moisture out of cheese.

Hamburger

Cross one palm over the other in front of your body. Squeeze your hands together as if you're shaping a ball of hamburger meat into a patty, then switch your hands so the bottom hand ends up on top.

Hot dog

With your palms facing down, touch your fists together, end to end. Then open your fists slightly, moving your hands outward, then bunch them into fists again, as if you're squeezing the ends of a hot dog.

Spaghetti

With your palms facing in toward your body, make an "I" handshape (see page 7) with each hand, pointing your pinkies toward each other. Then move your pinkies away from each other, making little curling motions as you go. To remember this sign, think of the curly noodles in spaghetti.

Milk

With your palm facing to the side, make a fist. Then squeeze it open and closed as if you are milking a cow.

Cereal

Make a "1" handshape (page 9) with your palm facing down, touch the side of your chin with your index finger, and then wiggle your finger side to side across your chin.

Water

With your palm facing to the side, make a "W" handshape (see page 8) and tap the side of your chin a couple of times as if you are bringing the edge of a cup to your face.

Juice

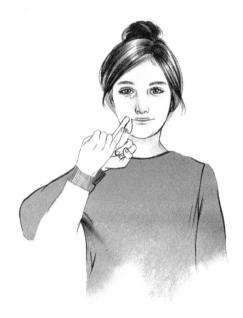

Using your pinkie finger, draw a small letter "J" on your cheek.

Ice cream

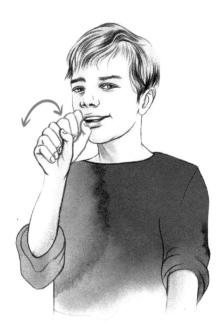

Hold your fist up to your mouth as if you're holding an ice-cream cone and move it up and down as if you are licking it!

Candy

With your palm facing out, hold your index fingertip up to your cheek and then twist your hand back and forth. To remember the sign, think of the dimple of a child's smile when someone gives them candy!

Deaf people love to talk!

If you ask a Child of a Deaf Adult (also known as CODA), they will tell you that Deaf people love to talk, and will talk for hours and hours! Sometimes restaurants have to politely ask Deaf patrons to leave when we stay well past closing and don't even realize that the restaurant is completely empty! Why do you think that is?

Imagine going to a foreign country where hardly anyone speaks English. Every day, you have to work extra hard to understand even a small portion of what is being communicated around you, because it's all in another language.

Now imagine how you feel when you finally get to meet with someone there who not only speaks English, but also grew up in the same area as you. You are excited to talk to them because suddenly you can communicate effortlessly. This person understands your journey, your culture, your language, and you can relate to them in so many ways.

This is how many Deaf people feel when they meet one another and converse in American Sign Language. So it's no surprise that Deaf people will sacrifice sleep and stay up late into the night to talk to one another!

8

The Great Outdoors

THIS IS ONE of my favorite chapters! Here you'll learn signs that relate to nature and the great outdoors. We'll cover some of nature's wonders like **FLOWER** and **GRASS**, weather such as **SNOW** and **LIGHTNING**, as well as the signs for the seasons. To practice these signs, go for a nature walk and try using signs to describe the weather and other things you see along your walk.

DID YOU KNOW

In the United States, a deaf person can obtain a driver's license after passing the standard driving tests. Most deaf people can drive very well—even while signing!

Outside/leave

With your palm facing in, make a "5" handshape (see page 9) near the upper side of your head. Bring all of your fingertips together in a pulling motion away from you. Do this twice. If you do this sign with just one pulling motion, it becomes the sign for **LEAVE**.

Nature

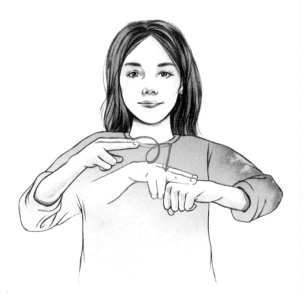

Hold both hands in front of you, palms facing down. Make a "U" handshape (see page 8) with your top hand and a closed fist with your bottom hand. Make a slight circular motion with your top hand, then bring it down to land your fingertips on the top of your fist, like a butterfly landing on your hand.

Tree

Hold one arm in front of you across your body with your hand out flat as if you're resting on a flat surface. Make a "5" handshape (see page 9) with your other hand and rest that elbow on top of your bottom hand. Twist your top hand at the wrist a few times as if shaking the branches of a tree.

Flower

With your palm facing to the side and slightly bent, bring all of your fingertips together and touch them to one side of your nose. Then rotate the fingers around your nose to touch them to the other side. To remember this sign, think of smelling flowers!

Grass

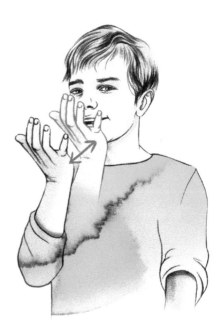

With your palm facing up, make a claw handshape and touch your palm to your chin a few times in an outward motion. To remember the sign, think of lying on your stomach in the grass and the blades sticking up around your face.

Sun

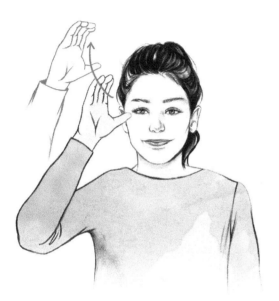

With your palm facing to the side, make a "C" handshape (see page 7) and touch it to the side of your face. Then raise your hand away from your head, like the sun rising into the sky.

Moon

This is very similar to the sign for **SUN**. With your palm facing to the side, make a "C" handshape (see page 7) with just your index finger and thumb. Touch your thumb to the side of your face and raise your hand up and away from your head, like a crescent moon rising.

Star

With your palms facing out, point both index fingers. Brush your index fingers against each other in an up and down movement, like you are pointing up at the stars.

Weather

With both hands facing out, make a "5" handshape (see page 9) with both hands and move them down in a squiggly motion, keeping your fingers straight.

Winter/cold

With your palms facing together, hold up both your fists in front of your chest. Shake your fists in and out as if you are shivering. To use this sign to say **COLD**, make a facial expression that shows you are freezing. If you're using this sign to say **WINTER**, then do not make a facial expression.

Spring/grow

With your palm facing to the side, make a loose fist in front of your body. With your other hand, touch all of your fingertips together, palm facing in, and push your hand through the open fist while opening up your fingers, like a flower blooming. Repeat this movement a few times. If you make this sign with just one movement, it is the sign for **GROW**.

Summer

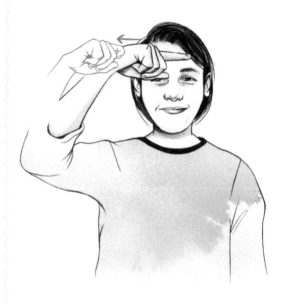

With your palm facing down, point your index finger and hold it up to the opposite side of your forehead. Then pull your index finger across your forehead as you bend it into an "X" handshape (see page 8), as if you are wiping sweat off your brow.

Autumn/fall

With your palm facing down, make a "5" handshape (see page 9) and brush your hand against the elbow of your opposite arm a few times, as if you're brushing leaves off the sleeve of your jacket.

Hot

With your palm facing in, make a claw handshape and cover your mouth. Then rotate your hand outward, away from your face, as if you are spitting out a bite of food that is too hot!

Rain

With your palms facing out, make a "5" handshape (see page 9) with both hands in front of your face. Drop your hands down at the wrist a few times, like falling raindrops.

Snow

This is almost like the sign for **RAIN** except you wiggle your fingers. With your palms facing out, make a "5" hand-shape (see page 9) with both hands in front of your face. Drop your arms down a few times while wiggling your fingers, like a flurry of snowflakes.

Wind

With your palms wide apart and facing each other, make a "5" handshape (see page 9) with both hands and sway your hands from side to side, like they are blowing in the wind.

? DID YOU KNOW

It is widely believed that many deaf people have enhanced vision to make up for their absence of hearing. They can often point out and remember very specific visual details that most hearing people would not even notice.

Thunder

Point to your ear with one index finger, then make fists with both hands, palms facing down. Shake your fists side to side, like you are a loud clap of thunder shaking the ground.

Lightning

With your palm facing out in a "1" handshape, use your index finger to draw a jagged line downward, as if you are drawing the shape of a lightning bolt.

Emergency services for the Deaf

Imagine being in an emergency situation and not being able to call for help. In the not-too-distant past, deaf people had to either be near a TTY/TDD (a typewriter phone device for the deaf that was mainly only found on a few select pay phones and in the homes of deaf people), or near a hearing person who could call for them.

One of the best advantages for the deaf/hard-of-hearing (hh) community has been texting. Many states and cities have improved emergency response services for the deaf by accepting 911 calls via text. This is especially helpful when there is not a strong enough cell signal to make an emergency Video Relay Service call (page 63).

Some states have registries for people who might need special assistance in emergency situations, such as extreme weather conditions. Deaf/hh people on these lists would be notified of important updates and instructions via text alerts rather than relying on phone calls and audio alerts. In these situations, it's important that safety news broadcasts are either closed captioned or interpreted by a qualified sign language interpreter.

9

School and Learning

SCHOOL IS A wonderful place to use signs, especially if you have Deaf/hard-of-hearing (hh) kids at your school. Maybe you've had teachers use signs in the classroom to quietly communicate simple requests, such as **BATHROOM** or **WATER**. Or maybe you've learned to sign a song for a music class or performance. There are lots of opportunities to sign at school, and it always helps to have a buddy you can practice with.

School

With your palms facing together and your hands in flat handshapes, hold both hands horizontally across the front of your body. Clap your top flat palm against your bottom flat palm a few times, as if you're clapping for getting a good grade!

Learn/student/person

To sign **LEARN**, hold out your hand in a flat handshape, palm facing up. Touch the fingertips of your other hand to your flat palm and pull them together in an upward movement as if you are pulling information out of a book. To turn this sign into **STUDENT**, after signing **LEARN**, immediately change both of your hands into flat handshapes side by side, palms facing together, and move them straight downward. (When signed on its own, this is the sign for **PERSON**.)

Study

Hold out one hand in a flat handshape with your palm facing up. With your other hand, make a "5" handshape (see page 9) and point your fingertips down at your palm and wiggle your fingers.

Read

With your palm facing up or to the side, hold out a flat handshape. With your other hand, make a "V" handshape (see page 8) and point your fingertips toward your flat palm. Drop your fingers down your palm, as if your fingertips are two eyes scrolling down the page of a book.

Write

With your palm facing up, hold out your hand in a flat handshape. With your other hand, hold your thumb and index finger together like you're holding a pencil and make a writing motion across your flat palm, just like you're writing something on a piece of paper.

? DID YOU KNOW

Many states have residential schools that serve Deaf/hard-of-hearing (hh) students throughout that state. One advantage to students attending these schools, rather than a mainstream school, is the fully inclusive environment of Deaf/hh peers, teachers, and staff.

History

With your palm facing to the side, make an "H" handshape (see page 7). Then move your hand up and down at the wrist in a chopping motion.

Math/algebra/geometry

With your palms facing together, make the "M" handshape (see page 8) with both hands, and place one hand slightly higher than the other. Moving your hands horizontally, brush your hands against each other a couple of times. If you make this sign with an "A" hand-shape, you have **ALGEBRA**, if you do it with a "G," you have **GEOMETRY**, and so on.

English

With the palm of one hand facing down, make a loose fist with your other hand and place it on top of your flat hand. Move both hands slightly inwards, towards your body.

Science

With your palms facing out, make an "A" handshape (see page 7) with both hands. Then move them alternately in a circular motion as if you were scrubbing a window.

? DID YOU KNOW

Deaf people who sign have accents just like hearing people. Region, education, background, personal signing style, and the age they learned sign language can all factor into someone's sign accent.

Language

With your palms facing down and thumbs almost touching, make an "L" handshape (see page 8) with both hands. Then move your hands away from each other out to the sides. This sign can also be done with "F" handshapes.

Technology

Hold up one hand in a flat handshape, horizontally, with your palm facing in. Then, with your other hand in a "5" handshape (page 9), tap the middle finger of your other hand to the bottom of your top hand a few times.

Gym

With your palms facing your body and fingers pointing up, make loose fists with both hands. Then make small circular motions with your hands and upper arms, as if you are jumping rope.

Teach/teacher

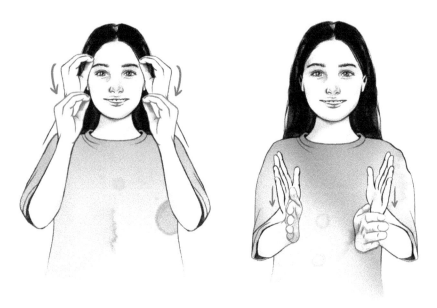

To sign **TEACH**, make a flat "O" hand-shape (see page 8) with both hands in front of your face, palms facing together, and move your hands out and down in a repeated movement. To turn this sign into **TEACHER**, immediately after signing **TEACH**, change your hands to flat handshapes, palms facing together and move them straight downward to sign **PERSON**.

Class

With your palms facing out, make a "C" handshape (see page 7) with both hands. Then circle your hands around in a forward motion until your palms are facing you, as if you are creating a bubble around a group of people.

Book

Hold up both hands in a flat handshape with your palms touching. Then open your palms while keeping the pinkie side of your hands touching, as if you are opening a book!

Library

With your palm facing out, make an "L" handshape (see page 8) and then move your hand in a circular motion.

Test

With your palms facing out, point your index fingers up and repeatedly bend them into "X" handshapes (see page 8) as you move your hands downward. The "wiggling X" handshape is often used to show a question in ASL, so think of a bunch of question marks running down a test sheet.

Homework

Close the fingertips of one hand together and bring them to your cheek as if you are going to sign **HOME** (page 32). With your other hand, make a fist out in front of you, palm facing down. Then change the handshape of your top hand into a fist and drop it down until you hit your bottom fist to make the sign for **WORK**.

Smart

With your palm facing to the side, tap your middle finger to your forehead, keeping the rest of your fingers straight. Then twist your hand until your palm is facing out.

How do you get the attention of a Deaf person?

When someone is across the room and you need to get their attention, what do you usually do? Let me guess—you call out their name. Well, what if they can't hear you? Deaf people have all sorts of creative ways to get each other's attention. They wave their hands in the air, tap each other on the shoulder, or stomp on the floor to create vibrations. Sometimes they flash the lights, throw something soft (like a crumpled piece of paper) into the person's line of sight, or ask someone who is closer to them to get their attention. Many of these methods may seem offensive to a hearing person, but they are perfectly acceptable in Deaf culture!

10

Descriptive Words

CONGRATS—YOU MADE IT to the final chapter! Can you believe how many signs you've learned in a short amount of time? Now we'll go over signs for descriptive words to help you communicate size, color, shape, and more. A heads-up: the signs for **SMALL**, **MEDIUM**, and **LARGE** have specific mouth shapes that you make along with the sign. Making these mouth shapes may feel a bit silly at first, but I assure you they are a natural part of the language and Deaf people use them all the time!

Deaf

With your palm facing to the side, touch your index finger near your mouth, then bring your finger up to touch near your ear.

Hearing

With your hand in a "1" handshape (see page 9) and palm facing down, touch your index finger just below your lip and make forward circular motions, like sounds coming out of your mouth.

Good

Hold out one hand in a flat handshape with your palm facing up. Touch the fingertips of your other flat hand to your mouth or chin, then bring that hand down to meet your other hand with both palms facing up.

Bad

This sign is similar to the sign for **GOOD**. Hold out one hand in a flat handshape with your palm facing up. Touch the fingertips of your other flat hand to your mouth or chin, then bring the hand down toward your bottom hand as if you are about to sign **GOOD**, but quickly flip your palm so it slaps onto your bottom palm to sign **BAD** instead.

Red

Touch the tip of your index finger to your chin and pull your finger downward into an "X" handshape (see page 8).

Yellow

With your palm facing in, make a "Y" handshape (see page 8) in front of you and twist your wrist so your palm turns out and in a few times.

Green

With your palm facing to the side, make a "G" handshape (see page 7) and twist your wrist so your palm turns out and in a few times.

Blue

With your palm facing in, hold up a
"B" handshape (see page 7) and twist
your wrist so your palm turns in and
out a few times.

Black

With your palm facing down, point your
index finger to the opposite side of your
forehead and drag the side of your
finger across your forehead in a line.

Brown/tan

With your palm facing out, make a
"B" handshape (page 7) and touch your
index finger to your cheek. Slide your
hand down the side of your face in a
straight line. If you do this sign with a
"T" handshape, it becomes the sign
for **TAN**.

White

With your palm facing in, start by
holding a "5" handshape (see page 9)
to your chest. Then close all of your
fingertips together as you pull the
hand away from your chest.

Purple

With your palm facing in, hold up a "P" handshape (see page 8) in front of your chest and rotate your wrist so your palm turns out and back a couple of times.

Orange

With your palm facing to the side, hold a fist up to your chin and open and close your fingers in a squeezing motion, just like you are squeezing juice from an orange.

Pink

With your palm facing in, make a "P" handshape (see page 8) and draw a small line down your chin with your middle finger. This movement can either be done once or twice.

Small

Make flat handshapes with both palms facing each other and move your hands in and out repeatedly without touching, as if you are showing the size of a small animal. When doing this sign, squeeze your lips into a tiny "o" shape, like you are saying "oooh."

Medium

Make both hands into flat handshapes with one slightly above the other. Face the top palm to the side and the bottom palm toward your body, pinkie-side down. With your top hand, make a small chopping motion into the middle part of your bottom hand. When you make this sign, purse your lips together tightly as if you are saying "Mmm."

Big/large

Hold your hands in front of your body, palms facing each other, and make an "L" handshape (see page 8) with both hands and your index fingers bent. Pull your hands away from each other as if you're showing something growing bigger. When you make this sign, move your mouth to look like you are saying "cha."

In addition to the basic handshapes, American Sign Language uses classifiers, which are rule-based handshapes and pantomimes that give more information about nouns and verbs.

? DID YOU KNOW

Deaf babies babble, too! If a baby who is Deaf is signed to from an early age, they will babble in sign just like hearing babies babble vocally. Babies can start signing as early as six months!

Square/circle/ triangle/ rectangle

Point both your index fingers forward and use them both to draw a square in the air in front of you. You also use your index fingers this way to draw other shapes like **CIRCLE**, **TRIANGLE**, and **RECTANGLE**.

Where do I go from here?

Have you enjoyed learning American Sign Language (ASL) as much as I have enjoyed sharing it with you? If you're interested in learning more, I have some great suggestions. Start by asking around and researching local ASL community groups, clubs, or activities. You might discover fun opportunities like ASL story times at libraries, special after school activities, or summer camps. You can check your local library for more ASL books and videos. There are also lots of ASL websites and apps to help you along your sign language journey. (See the Resources section, page 151, for some of my recommendations.)

But one of the best ways to become more fluent in ASL is to reach out and become friends with Deaf/hard-of-hearing (hh) kids. Deaf/hh people are generally very patient and accommodating toward hearing people who are learning ASL, and will be happy to slow down and teach you new signs as needed.

Another good thing to know is that there's a great demand in the professional world for people who are fluent in ASL, so knowing this language could help you get a job someday! Many high schools and universities offer ASL classes and degrees in ASL-related fields. The best thing to do is to keep practicing, so you are ready to sign whenever an opportunity shows up!

Resources

~~~~~~~~~~~~~

www.aslexpressions.com

www.wecansign.com

www.signingwithautism.com

www.nad.org

www.signingtime.com

www.handspeak.com/kid

www.asl-kids.com

www.lifeprint.com

The Gallaudet Children's Dictionary of American Sign Language. Washington, DC: Gallaudet University Press, 2014.

Index

Acknowledgments

Thank you to my parents for never letting me use my hearing loss as an excuse; for pushing me to break through barriers and always advocate for myself. Mom, when the doctor told you that I probably wouldn't graduate from high school, thank you for drying your tears, stubbornly disagreeing, and making it your personal mission to prove him wrong. To my father, thank you for challenging me to reach out to others, in spite of perceived communication barriers. You inspire me to build meaningful relationships and always see the good in others. You are right, Daddy, it *is* a beautiful day in the neighborhood.

Thank you, Jason, and my kids, Ashlie, Kerrie, Ellie, Braunsen and Rex, for being my adventure buddies and for putting up with my dreadful singing voice, disappointing culinary skills, and never-ending requests to stop everything and watch a sunset. Thank you for being my number-one fans, and sometimes having more faith in me than I have in myself.

Thank you, Jill Muir, the outreach consultant who encouraged my parents to introduce me to the world of signing and the Deaf community. You altered the course of my life and I will be forever grateful.

I would like to thank the teachers, administration, staff, and students at ISDB for creating a "Hogwarts world." Being there made me feel "normal" and taught me not to be ashamed of the magic of being Deaf.

Thanks also to my best friend, Emma, who has stuck around longer than anyone else, through good times and bad. Thank you for all the adventures we've had and the stories we will someday tell our grandkids (or not).

Thanks to my students, many of whom have become my closest friends and steadfast supporters. To Doris, Lana and Jeff, Angela, the O'Donnell family, Becky, Ruth and Frances, Dave, John, Eli and Estella, Dildines, Steve, Deseret, and so many more: You have left an imprint on my heart. I wouldn't be who I am today without you.

I would like to thank the entire team at Callisto Media for putting their faith in me.

I would especially like to thank Barbara Isenberg, the editor of this project, for her enthusiasm, encouragement, and incredible eye for detail. Her own personal background in the Deaf community and extensive knowledge of ASL and Deaf culture made her an invaluable co-creator of this project. I would also like to thank the illustrator, Natalia Sanabria, for creating the most beautiful illustrations I have ever seen in an ASL book.

Lastly, I want to thank anyone who is learning sign language so you can connect with someone who cannot hear or has difficulty communicating verbally. You are giving them an incredible gift.

About the Author

 **TARA ADAMS** began losing her hearing as a toddler. At age six, she was diagnosed with progressive hearing loss and by the time she was in middle school, her hearing loss was profound. Enrolling in the Idaho School for the Deaf and Blind changed her life: there, she found a community of kids just like her. Encouraged by their acceptance, she immediately pulled back her long hair, which previously had covered her hearing aids, into a ponytail. A passionate teacher was born.

Tara is the founder of ASL Expressions. She is an outspoken advocate of sign language not only for the Deaf, but also for individuals who struggle to communicate via spoken language. Tara recently founded SigningWithAutism.com and WeCanSign.com, both with the aim to spread awareness of sign language as a communication tool for nonverbal or speech-delayed children.

Printed in the USA
CPSIA information can be obtained
at www.ICGtesting.com
CBHW042135270124
3674CB00001B/6